THE *ENDURANCE* EXPEDITION

Essential Events

THE ENDURANCE
EXPEDITION
BY KRISTIN JOHNSON

Content Consultant
Laura Kissel, Polar Curator
Byrd Polar Research Center Archival Program,
Ohio State University

ABDO
Publishing Company

CREDITS

Published by ABDO Publishing Company, 8000 West 78th Street, Edina, Minnesota 55439. Copyright © 2011 by Abdo Consulting Group, Inc. International copyrights reserved in all countries. No part of this book may be reproduced in any form without written permission from the publisher. The Essential Library™ is a trademark and logo of ABDO Publishing Company.

Printed in the United States of America,
North Mankato, Minnesota
112010
012011

 THIS BOOK CONTAINS AT LEAST 10% RECYCLED MATERIALS.

Editor: Melissa York
Copy Editor: Amy E. Quale
Interior Design and Production: Kazuko Collins
Cover Design: Kazuko Collins

Library of Congress Cataloging-in-Publication Data
Johnson, Kristin.
   The Endurance expedition / by Kristin Johnson.
      p. cm. -- (Essential events)
   Includes bibliographical references and index.
   ISBN 978-1-61714-764-7
   1. Shackleton, Ernest Henry, Sir, 1874-1922--Travel--
Antarctica--Juvenile literature. 2. Endurance (Ship)--
Juvenile literature. 3. Imperial Trans-Antarctic Expedition
(1914-1917)--Juvenile literature. 4. Antarctica--Discovery and
exploration--Juvenile literature. I. Title.
   G850 1914 .S53 J65 2011
   919.8'904--dc22

                              2010043851

TABLE OF CONTENTS

The Endurance *set sail from England in August 1914.*

ON THIN ICE

During the nineteenth and early twentieth centuries, popular interest in Earth's polar regions was high. Explorers from all countries raced to accomplish milestones—first to the North Pole, first to the South Pole. Sir Ernest Shackleton of Ireland set himself the most difficult goal of all, seeking to be the first to cross the entire continent of Antarctica. On August 8, 1914, the ship the *Endurance* left England. Newspapers proclaimed:

> The *Endurance, with Sir Ernest Shackleton and the Imperial Trans-Antarctic Expedition on board, steamed away from the South India Dock pierhead on Saturday morning on the first stage of her journey to the Polar regions. . . . As the boat cast off from the pier and took the center of the river the crowds raised hearty cheers, which were acknowledged by Sir Ernest Shackleton.*[1]

After stopping in Argentina in October, the ship held expedition leader Sir Ernest Shackleton, a crew of 26 men, one stowaway, 69 Canadian sled dogs, and one cat. Shackleton's goal was to be the first to make the 1,800-mile (29,000-km) trek across Antarctica. At the time, the continent was the last uncharted territory on Earth—the unknown. In his "Expedition Prospectus," Shackleton had written, "From the sentimental point of view, it is the last great Polar journey that can be made."[2]

This would be Shackleton's third journey to Antarctica. Shackleton had tried twice previously to reach the South Pole but had failed in each attempt.

However, because he was the first man to get within 100 miles (160 km) of the South Pole, the king of England knighted him. He was thereafter known to the world as "Sir Ernest." To his crew members, who respected their savvy leader, he was simply "the Boss."

Sir Ernest was beaten in his attempts to reach the South Pole by fellow explorers Roald Amundsen of Norway and Robert Falcon Scott of the United Kingdom. They succeeded in their journeys to reach the bottom of Earth before him, gaining fame for themselves and national pride

Hiring the Crew

It is said that Shackleton placed this ad when looking for men for the journey: "Men wanted for hazardous journey. Small wages, bitter cold, long months of complete darkness, constant danger, safe return doubtful. Honour and recognition in case of success."[3]

Men were selected from an overwhelming pool of applicants based on the needs of the expedition. Surveyor Frank Wild, for example, was named second in command, and Captain Frank Worsley specialized in ramming or cutting through ice. The other men included surgeons, a carpenter, a photographer, an artist, engineers, navigators, a cook, scientists, and men who could help run the ship.

When the *Endurance* left port, 28 men were on board: the 26 Shackleton hired, Shackleton himself, and one stowaway, Perce Blackborrow. Shackleton confronted the 18-year-old Blackborrow and said, "Do you know that on these expeditions we often get very hungry, and if there is a stowaway available he is the first to be eaten?" The brave young Welshman joked to the heavyset Shackleton, "They'd get a lot more meat off you, sir."[4] Shackleton respected the boy's sense of humor and kept him on board, appointing him the cook's assistant.

for their respective countries. Shackleton wanted fame and fortune for himself. The expedition of 1914 with the *Endurance*, if successful, could redeem his reputation. More than that, Shackleton was restless. Regular life bored him. He needed to go south to feed his adventurous spirit.

Shackleton and his crew left England just as World War I (1914–1918) was beginning and sailed to Argentina. From there, they went on to South Georgia Island—their last stop for supplies before heading toward Antarctica. Before leaving South Georgia Island, Shackleton heard from local whalers that the pack ice was even rougher and more dangerous that year than usual. So the expedition waited several months for more favorable conditions, eventually taking off December 5, 1914, headed for the Weddell Sea. This was the height of the brief Antarctic summer, and the land was bathed in light almost around the clock.

"Shackleton's enemy was not the ice, but it was his own people, in the sense it was their morale. That was the foe. He had to prevent their morale from crumbling. The ice was nothing. Anybody can deal with the ice, but to deal with the human spirit—that is very difficult."[5]

—*Shackleton biographer Roland Huntford*

*The crew lived in Ocean Camp on the ice
after the* Endurance *was trapped.*

STRANDED

On January 19, 1915, less than two months after
the explorers left civilization, pack ice, or solid and
broken pieces of ice, closed in on the *Endurance*,
leaving the ship and its crew stuck on the frozen
Weddell Sea. Pack ice can crack apart suddenly,
creating life-threatening crevasses in the ice. This
danger left the crew of the *Endurance* constantly on
edge while living atop the ice.

The land mass of Antarctica was in view within 100 miles (160 km), but the *Endurance* was unable to move closer to its destination. Trapped, the crew waited to see if the ship would break free so they could continue their journey. They also tried to free the ship by breaking up the ice with ice picks, saws, and shovels. In the meantime, the crew used the lifeboats for shelter and set up their first camp on the icy tundra, dubbing it Ocean Camp.

In Ocean Camp, the men kept chipping away at the ice that surrounded the *Endurance*, but to no avail. The *Endurance* and its crew could not break free. The camp itself was pitched on an ice floe—a piece of floating ice. Because of the moving ground, Ocean Camp and the *Endurance* drifted, every day floating farther away from Antarctica. Soon, they were more than 500 miles (800 km) away from their destination on the continent.

To feed their hunger, the crew ate penguins and seals. To stay warm, they played soccer on the ice floe.

Pack Ice

Pack ice was the enemy of ships traveling into polar regions. Most of Antarctica's sea ice melts and refreezes each year. If pack ice surrounded a ship, as with the *Endurance*, the ship and its crew would be trapped for months. The crew could try to free their ship by chipping away at the ice with pick axes, but usually it was no use. Most likely, the ship was stuck waiting for warmer weather that might melt the thick ice.

To survive the wait, they sang songs and told stories. Shackleton knew that keeping the crew's spirits up was one of his greatest challenges. The waiting was the hardest part. They waited for the ice to loosen, hoping it would melt when warmer weather arrived. The brief summer ended, and the endless night of Antarctic winter closed in. They waited in Ocean Camp from January through October—ten long, cold months—but the *Endurance* remained trapped in the pack ice and continued to drift even farther away from land. The men still had hopes of crossing Antarctica, which was their original goal. They intended to camp on the ice only until the *Endurance* broke free, and then they planned to continue the mission.

The Pack Closes In

On October 27, 1915, the powerful pack ice surrounding the ship crushed the hull inward, destroying the *Endurance* beyond repair. "The end came at last about 5:00 p.m.—she was doomed, no ship built by human hands could have withstood the strain—I ordered all hands on to the floe and as the floe near us was cracking we started to sledge all the gear,"[6] wrote Shackleton. The crew stood by helplessly and watched their vessel being slowly snapped apart. The lifeboats and remaining rations and supplies were gathered and saved off the ship. This also destroyed the last hope Shackleton had of continuing on the original mission. They had drifted on the ice 573 miles (922 km) from where the *Endurance* had originally been stuck by the pack ice. Based on their remaining food and supplies, Shackleton determined that they should march across the ice 346 miles (557 km) to Paulet Island, the nearest piece of land. Shackleton knew the island would have food and shelter left over from a Swedish expedition in 1902.

At this point, the crew began its march across the ice. They strapped themselves into harnesses to drag the lifeboats one at a time. They used sledges to move the gear and lifeboats through snowdrifts, sinking frequently into the soft snow. This trek across the ice was slow; they often were only able to make one mile (1.6 km) in a day with all the supplies they carried. They moved the lifeboats and then camped at night,

"She has been strained, her beams arched upwards, by the fearful pressure; her very sides opened and closed again as she was actually bent and curved along her length, groaning like a living thing."[7]

—Captain Frank Worsley describing the destruction of the *Endurance*

The pack ice entirely crushed the Endurance.

sometimes going back to the ship in smaller groups
to retrieve loads of food.

Swallowed by the Sea

The slow destruction of the ship went on for
another month. They had made so little progress
that they were able to watch the ship through a

spyglass. Then, on November 21, 1915, the Boss called out to his men, "She's going, boys!"[8]

In his diary, the ship's captain, Frank Worsley, shared those last moments:

> She went down bows first, her stern raised in the air. She then gave one quick dive and the ice closed over her for ever. It gave one a sickening sensation to see it, for, mastless and useless as she was, she seemed to be a link with the outer world. Without her our destitution seems more emphasized, our desolation more complete. The loss of the ship sent a slight wave of depression over the camp. . . . The moment of severance . . . had come as she silently up-ended to find a last resting-place beneath the ice.[9]

After the *Endurance* disappeared beneath the surface of the Weddell Sea, Shackleton pronounced the death of their beloved ship, "She's gone, boys."[10]

As a result of the *Endurance* sinking, the crew faced a daring rescue mission: an 800-mile (1,300-km) open-boat journey in dangerous Antarctic waters to reach civilization. How did Shackleton get his men out

"It was a sickening sensation to feel the decks breaking up under one's feet, the great beams bending and then snapping with a noise like heavy gunfire. . . . I cannot describe the impression of relentless destruction that was forced upon me as I looked down and around. The floes, with the force of millions of tons of moving ice behind them, were simply annihilating the ship."[11]

—*Captain Frank Worsley*

of such dire circumstances? How did these men survive the blistering subzero temperatures? What did they use for food and shelter? This epic voyage was one of the last events of the age of heroic polar exploration. But the real accomplishment was in how every one of those 28 men came back from Antarctica alive.

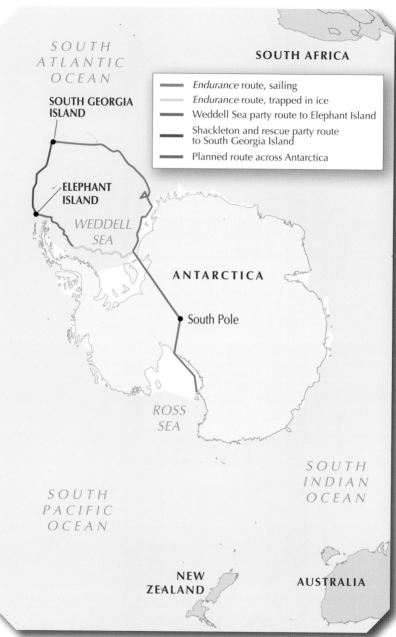

SOUTH
ATLANTIC
OCEAN

SOUTH AFRICA

**SOUTH GEORGIA
ISLAND**

	Legend
▬	*Endurance* route, sailing
▬	*Endurance* route, trapped in ice
▬	Weddell Sea party route to Elephant Island
▬	Shackleton and rescue party route to South Georgia Island
▬	Planned route across Antarctica

**ELEPHANT
ISLAND**

*WEDDELL
SEA*

ANTARCTICA

● South Pole

*ROSS
SEA*

*SOUTH
INDIAN
OCEAN*

*SOUTH
PACIFIC
OCEAN*

**NEW
ZEALAND**

AUSTRALIA

The Endurance *and Weddell Sea party route*

For his entire life, Ernest Shackleton sought adventure.

THE BOSS

Ernest Henry Shackleton was born in Kilkea, County Kildare, Ireland, on February 15, 1874. He was the second oldest of ten children. All of his siblings were girls except one younger brother, Frank. Ernest and his family lived in Dublin, Ireland, and he was homeschooled until the age of 11. Then, his father, who was a doctor, moved the family to London, England. In London, Ernest was sent to Dulwich College to study.

His father had hoped Ernest would follow in his footsteps and become a doctor, but Ernest did not excel at school. He was bored with it. He also was not interested in playing sports like his peers. He wanted adventure.

Destined for the Sea

When he was only 16 years old, Ernest left school and enlisted in the merchant marine. The merchant marine was a branch of the United Kingdom's Royal Navy. The ships of the merchant marine carried important cargo for the nation. Ernest became a sailor, and the first ship he served on was the British merchant ship *Hoghton Tower*. It was on those voyages that Ernest began to look south and form his dreams of polar exploration.

In 1897, Ernest was on shore leave when he was introduced to one of his sisters' friends, Emily Dorman. Emily was six years older than Ernest. He fell in love with Emily immediately. The biggest difference between them was that Emily was focused

on home and family life, but Ernest was what one of
his teachers called "a rolling stone."[1] Emily's father
did not approve of the relationship, yet they became
engaged. They had a prolonged engagement and saw
each other between Ernest's sea excursions.

SHACKLETON'S FIRST EXPEDITION

By 1898, at the age of 24, Shackleton became
a certified master, which enabled him to lead any
British ship on the sea. However, he still lacked his
own ship to command. In May 1900, Robert Falcon
Scott, a British Royal Navy captain, was planning
an expedition. Shackleton read the announcement
in the *Times* in London. Anxious to head south,
Shackleton immediately volunteered for the
excursion, which was called the National Antarctic
Expedition. At the time, Shackleton knew nothing
about Scott's leadership style or what it meant to be
the leader of such an expedition.

Once Shackleton was on the expedition and
aboard the ship *Discovery* in 1901, he learned just how
different he and Scott were from each other. Scott
was more stoic than Shackleton, and he led his men
like the navy captain he was. Because of this military
background, Scott believed that some loss of life was

acceptable in order for the mission to succeed. In contrast, Shackleton would later prove that he would rather fail in his expedition than lose a crew member's life.

On this expedition, Shackleton became very ill, coming down with scurvy—a sickness caused by a vitamin C deficiency. Shackleton changed his diet and began eating fresh meat rather than meat stored in tins. Fortunately for Shackleton, some vitamin C is present in fresh meat, especially liver meat, and he was able to recover. However, because scurvy affects the legs, among other things, Shackleton was temporarily disabled, and he had to be pulled on a sled. Early in 1903, Scott ordered Shackleton to go home early—against Shackleton's wishes. Shackleton was not one to fight in public, and he went home as commanded, promoting the success of the mission and its progress. This spirit of cooperation helped him later when he needed to raise funds for his own expeditions.

Ernest Shackleton and Emily Doran had married on April 9, 1901, shortly before Shackleton left on the *Discovery*. Upon his return from Antarctica,

The Nimrod *Expedition reached within 100 miles (160 km) of the South Pole before turning back.*

Shackleton settled into married life and spent some time as a journalist. His writing skills would prove useful later when he wrote several books on polar exploration. Shackleton had also published the *South Polar Times* while on the *Discovery* journey with Scott. Shackleton seemed skilled at whatever he tried. Throughout his life, he was a popular lecturer on polar exploration. He used his public speaking skills, especially early on, creating admirers while sharing his experiences on the *Discovery*. This included work with the Scottish Geographic Society, making speeches, and running for Parliament in 1905 (though he lost the election).

Shackleton and his wife eventually had three children, but they never reconciled their differences in lifestyles, and thus spent many years apart while Shackleton explored the Antarctic. He even promised Emily after each exploration that he would never go back, but he broke those promises when the sea called to him again. In the end, she accepted his repeated expeditions.

THE RACE FOR THE SOUTH POLE

In August 1907, Shackleton left England with his first crew on a ship called the *Nimrod*. Their goal was to be the first to reach the South Pole. Shackleton trusted his men with responsibility, and the crew respected him so much that they named him "the Boss." The name carried over into his other expeditions and throughout the rest of his life.

The expedition failed, getting within 97 miles (156 km) of the South Pole before turning back on

Nimrod Expedition Accomplishments

The *Nimrod* Expedition did not complete its main goal, but the crew had other achievements, such as climbing Mount Erebus, a volcano 12,448 feet (3,794 m) high. They also reached the magnetic South Pole on January 16, 1909, which proved an important scientific breakthrough. The north needle in every compass points to the magnetic North Pole and away from the magnetic South Pole. It is different from the geographic South Pole, which is the southern point around which Earth rotates.

January 9, 1909. The men were running low on provisions and would have died had they gone any farther. When the expedition returned to England, the king knighted Shackleton for being the first man to get that close to the South Pole.

Soon after, Scott made another bid to reach the South Pole. Rather than fuel a bitter rivalry, Shackleton offered to help prepare provisions for Scott. However, another explorer was also competing for the prize. The Norwegian explorer Roald Amundsen set a course for a five-year trek across the North Pole, but he changed plans at the last minute and admitted he was actually vying for the South Pole.

In the end, it was not Scott but Amundsen who was the first to reach the South Pole, claiming victory for Norway on December 14, 1911. One month later, Scott also reached the South Pole, but without the fanfare of being the first expedition to arrive.

After Shackleton was beaten by Amundsen and then Scott, he was still drawn to further exploration. With the quest for the South Pole over, Shackleton saw only one last great polar expedition—to trek 1,800 miles (2,900 km) across the entire continent. He believed there were many scientific discoveries to be made on the trip.

Emily begged him not to go back; after all, he had promised there would be no more expeditions. Each trip had left him physically and mentally spent. Once again he convinced her that he had to go back. He argued that because his accomplishments had been eclipsed, his days earning a living as a public speaker were over. In the end, Emily did not stand in his way.

As Shackleton began preparing for the trip, two tragedies occurred. First, the massive passenger ship *Titanic* sank when it struck an iceberg in April 1912, killing more than 1,500 people in the Atlantic Ocean. The second tragedy occurred in the South Pole: Scott and four members

A Matter of Life and Death

Norwegian explorer Roald Amundsen was the first person to reach the South Pole. English explorer Robert Falcon Scott reached the South Pole a month after Amundsen. Both gave their lives to their countries to further polar exploration. On Scott's 800-mile (1,300-km) return trip on foot from the South Pole, Scott's party was forced to camp. Scott, along with a few members of his party, froze to death at the end of March 1912. Scott was so dedicated to reaching his goals that he wrote diary entries even up until his death, recording scientific findings about plant life and weather in the Antarctic. His last diary entry, however, shows that he knew the end was near: "Had we lived, I should have had a tale to tell of hardihood, endurance, and courage of my companions." Scott's very last entry said, "It seems a pity, but I do not think I can write more."[3]

In 1928, Amundsen died while on a rescue mission searching for a fellow explorer whose airship had crashed while returning from the North Pole. Amundsen's rescue plane crashed in the sea. Rescuers found wreckage from his plane, but his body was never found.

of his expedition died in Antarctica, unable to escape the bitter elements. Shackleton declared this a tragedy and great loss for exploration.

Perhaps these tragedies shaped Shackleton's future explorations, fueling his belief in the need for careful planning. The polar regions were strewn with dead bodies of explorers. Shackleton even dubbed himself "Old Cautious."[4] He liked gaining that reputation, and it worked to his advantage. Polar exploration was expensive, and expedition leaders had to convince wealthy benefactors to pay for their journeys. It was better to be known as being cautious with others' money than being known as reckless.

With two failed expeditions behind him, Shackleton started planning the Trans-Antarctic Expedition. He proposed to cross the continent in his biggest adventure yet.

Testifying about *Titanic*

The passenger ship *Titanic* hit an iceberg late during the night of April 14 and sank on April 15, 1912. Shackleton was called on to testify in federal court in the United States on June 19 because he was an expert on ice and icebergs. The court was investigating who was at fault for the fatal sinking. His testimony put some blame on the ship's captain. Shackleton testified that the *Titanic* was traveling too quickly. He also said that icebergs can be seen from five miles (8 km) away on a clear night, implying that the iceberg should have been spotted in time to avoid the collision.

Shackleton's wife, Emily

Explorers have been drawn to Antarctica since the eighteenth century.

ORGANIZING THE
EXPEDITION

*I*n 1909, Shackleton wrote about his drive
for the Antarctic in his first book *The Heart
of the Antarctic: The Farthest South Expedition: 1907–1909*. Of
his second expedition south, on his ship *Nimrod*, he
said, "Men go out into the void spaces of the world

for various reasons . . . love of adventure . . . thirst for scientific knowledge, and . . . the mysterious fascination of the unknown."[1]

PULL OF THE POLE

As early as the sixteenth century, there was speculation about a continent existing in the southern regions at the South Pole. Governments were eager to send their explorers to lay claim to those new lands. Some of those earliest explorers of the region were Captain James Cook, who voyaged from 1773 to 1775; James Weddell, who led a sealing expedition in February 1823; and James Clark Ross, who reached the magnetic North Pole on May 31, 1831, and also sought the magnetic South Pole. The magnetic poles are the locations to which compasses point—the north needle points to the North Pole and the south needle points to the South Pole. These points are not the same as the geographic poles, which are the points where Earth turns on its axis.

Many of the regions and animals were named after the men who discovered them. The Weddell Sea and Weddell seals were named for James Weddell. The Ross Sea was named for James Clark Ross because he was the first to claim the region.

By the time Shackleton came along, land had been discovered but still not explored. The territory was yet uncharted, leaving plenty of the adventure Shackleton sought.

PLANNING AND FINANCING THE TRIP

Shackleton had already been planning his expedition for seven months, since mid-1913, before he made any formal announcements. He opened an office and placed an announcement in the *Times* in London on January 13, 1914. He also needed to find the proper ship—a ship that could withstand the elements and plow through the pack ice they would inevitably encounter.

Antarctic Seals

The Weddell seal was named for British sealing captain James Weddell in the 1820s. It can weigh up to 1,000 pounds (454 kg). Weddell seals are also the most approachable seals, so more is known about them than other species of seals. Later, in the 1840s, a different seal variety was named for Captain James Clark Ross. Ross seals are less common and are noted for their very large eyes.

Other Antarctic seals that Shackleton's expedition ran into were the crabeater seal and the leopard seal. A leopard seal nearly cost ski and sledge expert Tom Orde-Lees his life. One day, while Orde-Lees was out hunting for food, a leopard seal jumped out of a pool of water and onto the ice. Orde-Lees was nearly bitten by the huge mammal. He yelled for help, and crewmember Frank Wild came to the rescue and shot the animal. They ate it that night for dinner. The men ate the seals for survival and used their oil for fuel in cooking.

Eventually he purchased the *Endurance*. He also bought the *Aurora*, another whaling ship, to be used by a second party of men that would lay caches of supplies for the main group.

One of Shackleton's biggest challenges was raising enough money for the rest of his provisions and crew. Shackleton was so sure the excursion would happen that he began planning before he had the money. His enthusiasm and sureness that the voyage would go on helped make it happen.

The British government promised £10,000 for the trip as long as the other funds were secured first, and the Royal Geographic Society contributed £1,000. After gathering money from various sources, the last of the funds was secured within a month of leaving for the trip through a generous contribution of £24,000 by Scotsman James Caird. In thanks, the largest of the lifeboats was named

A New Name

The *Endurance* was originally called *Polaris*, but Shackleton renamed the ship after an old family motto, Fortitudine Vincimus, which means "By endurance we conquer."[2] The ship was built for Norwegian whaling captain Lars Christensen. His plan was to take tourists on cruises where they could hunt for polar bears. When his business plans fell through, Christensen sold the ship to Shackleton.

after him. In 2010, Shackleton's trip of £60,000 would equal more than $6 million in US funds.

Shackleton was able to get donations for the trip because of his persuasiveness as a speaker and his perseverance as a leader. People wanted to be sure their donations were well spent on an expedition that was likely to be successful. This is the reason Caird gave for donating so much money. Any less, and there would not have been enough money for the mission to be completed. Shackleton finally had the money needed to fund the voyage.

Naming the Lifeboats

The lifeboats were named after the three main monetary contributors to the expedition: *Stancomb-Wills, Dudley Docker,* and *James Caird.* The £24,000 donation by James Caird was the final money Shackleton needed to make the voyage happen, so he named the biggest lifeboat after Caird.

HIRING AN OPTIMISTIC CREW

Shackleton looked for four main qualities in the men he hired: optimism, patience, imagination, and courage. Initially, he selected key members for his crew from men he had worked with in the past or men he knew had the fortitude for such a journey. He had worked with six of the men on previous journeys, including Frank Wild. One of the first

Shackleton chose men for his crew who could get along in close quarters.

men chosen for the expedition, Wild was placed second in command of the *Endurance*. Shackleton had also worked with Wild during his first Antarctic journey on the *Discovery*.

One of the most unusual stories of those hired was that of Captain Frank Worsley. He claimed to have dreamed about sailing down a street in London. The next day he walked on that same street and saw Shackleton's headquarters for the Imperial Trans-Antarctica Expedition. Worsley walked right in to

Frank Hurley, Photographer and Filmmaker

Frank Hurley was hired as the expedition photographer. At the time, he was the most renowned filmmaker in the business. He had already successfully filmed other expeditions in polar regions. Conveniently, the *Endurance* had a darkroom built into it when Shackleton bought the ship. Later, when the *Endurance* was sinking, Hurley went back to the ship and risked his life by swimming into a partially sunken cabin to fish out his negative plates and save some of the footage he had shot. He then negotiated with Shackleton in order to bring 150 of the heavy glass plates on the long journey home.

apply for a job, and he was hired on the spot.

Shackleton received 5,000 responses to his ad for crew members—and he needed only 26 men. The responses were sorted into three piles: "Mad, Hopeless, and Possible."[3] Of the "possible" applications, only 56 applicants were interviewed.

During the interviews, Shackleton asked unexpected questions. For example, he wanted to know if the men sang. He was trying to find out how well they would get along together and if they had the resilience to persevere through the rougher elements of Antarctic exploration. They would face extremely cold weather and possibly long periods of waiting. How would the men entertain themselves during desperate times? Shackleton knew he would need men who could stay positive amid dire circumstances. Explorers had gone crazy in the Antarctic, and many had died.

The Boss knew the lonely life at sea. He was familiar with how difficult the waiting could be. He chose men who were optimists and who would be entertaining to travel with. Those qualities were just as important as skills and experience (if not more important) for surviving the desolation of the Antarctic.

A Tale of Two Sea Parties

Shackleton organized his expedition into two parties: the Weddell Sea party and the Ross Sea party. The Weddell Sea party would approach Antarctica via the Weddell Sea, land on the continent, and then cross Antarctica from shore to shore—a feat that had never been done before. The Weddell Sea party would have enough food to cross half of the continent. At the same time, the Ross Sea party would land

Endurance Facts

- Purchase Price to Shackleton: £11,000, approximately US$(2010) 1.2 million
- Length: 144 feet (44 m) long
- Weight: 350 tons (318 t)
- Construction Materials: Oak and Norwegian fir planks, covered on the outside with greenheart, a type of hardwood
- Where Built: Norway
- Designer: Ole Aanderud Larsen
- Powered By: Coal-fired steam and sail

on the other side of Antarctica and set up food depots for the second half of the Weddell Sea party's crossing of the continent. The depots would be laid approximately every 60 miles (100 km) from the edge of the Ross Sea to the South Pole.

The *Endurance*, the main expedition ship, was captained by Worsley. It would carry the Weddell Sea party, Shackleton, and the rest of the crew. The second ship, the *Aurora*, captained by Aeneas Mackintosh, would carry the Ross Sea party and the ship's crew, coming at Antarctica from the opposite side of the continent.

The Ross Sea party also had scientific goals, similar to other polar expeditions of the time, including magnetic, biological, and meteorological research. The Ross Sea party consisted of a small party that would go ashore and set up the depots and another group that would stay onboard and run the ship. ⌐

Shackleton left these canned goods behind in Antarctica on his Nimrod Expedition. He took similar goods on the Endurance Expedition.

*The men played soccer to exercise and keep their spirits up.
The* Endurance *is visible in the background.*

CAMPING ON THE ICE

hile the Ross Sea party set about laying food depots on the Ross Sea side of Antarctica, Shackleton and his men approached Antarctica from the opposite side through the Weddell Sea. But only two months into the journey the *Endurance* was stuck—trapped in the pack ice. Shackleton and his men struggled to free the *Endurance* for ten long months but had no way of getting word of this struggle to the men of the Ross Sea party, who kept rushing to lay food depots to ensure Shackleton's survival and successful crossing of Antarctica. Little did they know that Shackleton and his men never even set foot on the continent because they were trapped on the ice floe.

Part of the Weddell Sea party's survival relied on setting up camp on the ice when the *Endurance* became too unstable to stay aboard. Those camps, however, had to be easy to move in case the ice cracked and endangered the lives of the men. Of those moving camps, three were given names: Dump Camp, Ocean Camp, and Patience Camp.

Dump Camp was where they left nonessential personal belongings

Necessary for Survival

Once Shackleton knew they would lose the *Endurance* and would have to travel by sledge, he had the men dump any possessions not necessary for survival. However, Shackleton permitted the men to keep photographs and items to remind them of home. Shackleton reasoned, "A man under such conditions needs something to occupy his thoughts, some tangible memento of his home and people beyond the seas. So [money was] thrown away and photographs were kept."[1]

before marching across the ice. The meteorologist
Leonard Hussey was allowed to keep his banjo
because Shackleton called it essential to the morale
of the men. The rest of the men were told they could
take only two pounds (1 kg) of possessions with them
in search of Paulet Island, the nearest land and food
location known. Any more weight would hinder
their progress. They were told to only bring items
that would aid in eventual survival. Shackleton set
an example by tossing money, which was worthless
in the Antarctic, onto the snow. He even took the
Bible presented to him by Queen Alexandra and
tore out just a few pages to bring along. He kept one
page the queen had written on and another page
from the book of Job, an Old Testament story about
Job's unfailing faith in the face of extreme suffering.
Later, Shackleton would learn one of the men had
rescued the rest of the Bible. Shackleton also ordered
that the expedition's cat and three of the smallest
pups be shot because they would not survive the rest
of the journey. Chippy McNeish, the cat's owner,
never forgave Shackleton for the order.

After the *Endurance* sank on November 21, 1915,
they had to wait for the ice to break up so they could
launch the lifeboats. They needed open water and

warmer temperatures. The days were filled with waiting and strict routines, which were vital to keep the men focused.

Ocean Camp

The next main camp the men named was Ocean Camp. Daily activities of the camp included sending small parties out on foot to hunt seals and penguins for fresh food. Frank Wild, the second in command, coordinated the hunting efforts from camp. When food was found, a sock or scarf was used to signal Wild back at camp. Then Wild would signal back and come with a team of dogs to shoot and collect the animal.

At night the men took turns in one-hour shifts to watch the weather and look for signs the ice was cracking. They were sleeping on ice that was only five feet (1.5 m) thick. The dogs became especially weary

Sleeping Bags

Some of the crew slept in ten-pound (4.5-kg) reindeer-fur sleeping bags. The rest of the crew had less insulating wool sleeping bags. When the *Endurance* sank, there was a lottery system to determine who would get the 18 warmer reindeer bags. When they drew lottery numbers, Shackleton and the other officers drew for the colder wool bags, while their men all received the much warmer reindeer bags. Several of the men wrote in their diaries that they suspected the lottery was rigged and that Shackleton and his officers had made this sacrifice for the men serving under them. Shackleton was known for putting the needs of his men before his own, and the men respected him all the more for it. Shackleton later admitted in his memoir, "Some of us older hands did not join in the lottery."[2]

during the long nights and howled and cried with the wind. Even though the days with blizzard conditions were tougher, the men hoped for blizzards because it meant they would drift faster to Paulet Island than if the wind was calm. Because the ice was always threatening to break and swallow the men as it had swallowed the *Endurance*, Shackleton ran emergency drills, practicing packing and launching the boats within five minutes. The drills went well, and the idea of leaving the ice lifted the men's spirits.

Reading was also a daily occupation. They had part of the *Encyclopedia Britannica*, poetry by Robert Browning, "The Rime of the Ancient Mariner" by Samuel Coleridge, and books about polar exploration. The men would engage in lively discussions. If arguments ensued, they were often settled by looking in the encyclopedia. Two of their favorite topics to discuss were the weather and the rate at which they were drifting on the ice. They hoped the drift would work in their favor and move them closer to Paulet Island. Shackleton wrote about his strategy, "Our hope, of course, was to drift northwards to the edge of the pack and then, when the ice was loose enough, to take to the boats."[3]

The crew pulled the heavy lifeboats with them across the ice.

By December 20, Shackleton decided the weather was warm enough that they should drag the lifeboats to get closer to a point where they could launch them and row for land. In honor of this, the men celebrated Christmas Day early with a feast on December 22. They ate the best and biggest meal they had had since being marooned because they would not be able to carry all of the food with them on the long journey. Their feast consisted of anchovies cooked in oil, a traditional dish called jugged hare (stewed meat cooked in the animal's blood), and baked beans.

On the March

By December 23, the crew was marching in search of open water. The men kept moving and marched each day toward land. Shackleton felt that staying in place and waiting to be rescued would be more discouraging for the men than actively trying to improve their situation.

At the front of the procession were the stove and cooking utensils, followed by the dogs and then two of the boats. They had left the *Stancomb Wills* boat back at Ocean Camp. The march was slow, and the boats were heavy. Each boat weighed more than one ton (0.9 metric tonnes), including gear and the sledge used to drag the boats. In many places, the ice was hilly with steep ridges, making the already difficult task of dragging the lifeboats even worse. Soft snow was also hard to trudge through as the men often fell in up to their knees. Occasionally, the ice would be melted, and a man would dip into the water. Harnesses were attached to each man so he could be yanked up and saved when this occurred.

One of the men wrote about those days:

It's a hard, rough, jolly life, this marching and camping; no washing of self or dishes, no undressing, no changing of clothes. We have our food anyhow, and always impregnated with blubber-smoke; sleeping almost on the bare snow and working as hard as the human physique is capable of doing on a minimum of food.[4]

PATIENCE CAMP

On December 29, the Weddell Sea party stopped marching and set up Patience Camp. They built an igloo using ice blocks so the cook would have a kitchen. Because of the shortage of food, Shackleton had to order all dogs shot except for two teams. He felt awful about this; the dogs were working animals, but they were also

Sled Dogs and Ponies

In Shackleton's first expedition with the *Discovery*, Scott took dogs and skis. However, the English were not accustomed to using dogs as working animals, so the dogs were not utilized well. On his second expedition, on the *Nimrod*, Shackleton brought a combination of ponies, sled dogs, and a motorcar. The ponies ate hay, which had to be carried, whereas dogs could feed off the land and eat seals and penguins, just like the men. The motorcar failed in the freezing weather.

When Shackleton set south for his third time, with the *Endurance*, he reverted to bringing only sled dogs. The 69 Canadian sled dogs lived on the deck of the ship in kennels. So many dogs in close proximity created frequent barking and howling and occasional scuffles among the dogs. Later, when the *Endurance* became icebound and the crew had to abandon ship to live on the ice floe, igloos were built for the animals. The dogs provided irreplaceable companionship for the men during their long time trapped on the ice. Sadly, none of the dogs of the *Endurance* survived, but three dogs from the Ross Sea party lived. The rest were shot for food or killed when conditions would not permit humane existence.

companions for the men. But everything he did had to aid in the survival of the crew. When possible, Shackleton sent men back to Ocean Camp to retrieve more supplies that had been discarded. They had not carried everything with them on the sledging journey because the weight of the gear and lifeboats had made it impossible. Food was essential, so they went back for more of it when they could. They also reclaimed the third lifeboat.

In the interest of morale, Shackleton varied the menu served each week so the men would have something to think about. One man wrote of the rations:

> We are now very short of blubber, and in consequence one stove has to be shut down. We only get one hot beverage a day, the tea at breakfast. For the rest we have iced water. Sometimes we are short even of this, so we take a few chips of ice in a tobacco-tin to bed with us. In the morning there is about a spoonful of water in the tin, and one has to lie very still all night so as not to spill it.[5]

With a diet consisting of mostly penguin and seal, there was not one case of scurvy among the men. Still, these meals did not lead to a well-balanced diet and left the men feeling weak. Along with the poor diet, the weather was a constant hindrance to the campers. One man wrote in his diary of how the windy conditions affected Patience Camp:

> *The temperature was not strikingly low as temperatures go down here, but the terrific winds penetrate the flimsy fabric of our fragile tents and create so much draught that it is impossible to keep warm within. At supper last night our drinking-water froze over in the tin in the tent before we could drink it. It is curious how thirsty we all are.*[6]

Another man wrote in a journal: "One cannot suck ice to relieve the thirst, as at these temperatures it cracks the lips and blisters the tongue. Still, we are all very cheerful."[7]

In addition to being thirsty, by April 9, 1916, their food rations became scarce. Animals to hunt were few and far between. The penguins and seals had gone in search of food

Daily Food Rationing

In Ocean Camp, one man wrote in his diary: "Day by day goes by, much the same as one another. We work; we talk; we eat. . . . All is eaten that comes to each tent and everything is most carefully and accurately divided into as many equal portions as there are men in the tent. One member then closes his eyes or turns his head away and calls out the names at random, as the cook for the day points to each portion, saying at the same time, 'Whose?'"[8]

elsewhere. And with no radio or rescue airplanes at the time, no one was coming to help the men. No provisions would be dropping from above. All told, the crew had been drifting on the ice for more than a year. It was becoming clear they would have to leave the Antarctic region soon, or they would die. ⌐

Shackleton and his men relied on dogs for their survival.

The expedition headed for rocky and inhospitable Elephant Island.

OFF TO ELEPHANT ISLAND

On April 9, 1916 at 1:00 p.m., the 28-man crew of the *Endurance* loaded the lifeboats and pushed their way out through the pack ice surrounding Antarctica. They had drifted hundreds of miles on the ice floe. Paulet Island was no longer their best bet for survival. The whaling station at South Georgia Island was an 800-mile (1,300-km) journey—too far for the three lifeboats to cross on stormy waters. Instead, Shackleton set them on the shorter course for Elephant Island, the closest piece of land from the ice floe. This would only be a 60-mile (97-km) journey, so they had a much better chance of success. From there, Shackleton would take one boat and go on for help to South Georgia Island, risking fewer lives with a much smaller rescue party.

"We all shoved off . . . everyone felt very fit and full of hope, but the attempt to break out of the pack [ice] in such small boats must fill the most fearless with apprehension."[1]

—*Diary of Thomas Orde-Lees, ski and motor-sledge expert*

ON UNSTABLE GROUND

The men began their journey to Elephant Island. They rowed by day and then camped on ice floes at night. On April 9, Shackleton could not sleep and lay awake thinking. He remembered the night in his memoir:

Some intangible feeling of uneasiness made me leave my tent about 11 p.m. that night and glance around the quiet camp.

. . . As I was passing the men's tent the floe lifted on the crest of a swell and cracked right under my feet. The men were in one of the dome-shaped tents, and it began to stretch apart as the ice opened.[2]

A four-foot (1.2-m) crack widened in one spot. Seaman Ernie Holness was still inside his sleeping bag when he fell in. Shackleton quickly pulled Holness and the sleeping bag out of the freezing water to safety. Shortly after, movement in the ice floe slammed the two chunks of ice back together. That would have meant certain death for Holness had Shackleton not yanked him out of the water. No one slept after that. Orcas lurked in the water and blew spouts when they surfaced. The treacherous ice and the eerie noises kept the men on high alert throughout the night.

By 3:00 a.m., the blubber stove was heated up, and everyone enjoyed some hot milk. At 6:30 a.m. for breakfast, each man had hot hoosh, which is stew made with a mixture of dried meat, suet, and fat. By 8:00 a.m., the pack ice broke open,

"Ghostly Shadows"

Shackleton noted the feeling of being on the water late at night in his memoir *South*: "Occasionally the ghostly shadows of silver, snow, and fulmar petrels flashed close to us, and all around we could hear the killers [killer whales] blowing, their short, sharp hisses sounding like sudden escapes of steam."[3]

Spouting orcas scared Shackleton and his men in the night, but the whales are not known to harm humans in the wild.

allowing the men to launch the boats again. But soon the sea water sprayed over the men, covering them and their gear with freezing ice. Shackleton directed the boats to head back onto the pack ice because they could not survive the freezing conditions on the water that day. So they camped on an ice floe for another night and waited.

On the morning of April 11, they waited on the ice for their next move. The crew was strained from the stressful night, the freezing seawater, and 36 hours of exhausting rowing. Shackleton searched

the sea of ice in all directions, sometimes noting
the dark line in the distance indicating open water.
But they needed a closer place to launch the boats.
Shackleton reflected in his memoir about the
pressure he was under: "I do not think I had ever
before felt the anxiety that belongs to leadership
quite so keenly."[4]

By noon, the iceberg had drifted, the pack ice
cleared away, and the open water was closer. The
men threw their gear and what was left of their
provisions into the boats and shoved off once again.
At dusk, they found a heavy floe and stopped to camp
for the night. The men had hot milk and a cold
meal. They hoped to turn in for the night, but pack
ice surrounded the floe, and the men had to leave
or risk becoming trapped inside the pack ice once
again. With no land in sight, there was no rest for the
men. They pushed off and yelled back and forth in
the boats so they could stay close to each other in the
blackness of night. The orcas made the men anxious.
All it would take was one whale surfacing to knock
into one of the boats and capsize it.

The next day, the weather was better. It was less
windy, and the crew was even cheerful. The breakfast
of hot milk and Bovril (a kind of beef tea, similar to

a broth when mixed with water) was a welcome treat. The optimism the men showed for even a simple hot meal was what Shackleton had sought when hiring the crew. This positive spirit was what would help them get out alive. Other crews had been driven mad on polar expeditions. Shackleton was determined not to have that happen. The men camped again on a floe.

The next day, Captain Worsley took measurements to determine their progress. Sadly, the men had drifted 30 miles (48 km) southeast, instead of westward as they had hoped. Shackleton, Worsley, and Wild agreed not to share the truth with the

Killer Whales

Killer whales can grow to be more than 25 feet (7.6 m) long. They swam about the boats as the men made their way through the pack ice. Captain Worsley noted the incredible size of one of these whales by its belly: "It has been recorded that one, after being harpooned and cut up, contained twelve seals and ten porpoises! It need hardly be said that we gave thin ice a wide berth when killers were about."[5]

The scientific name for these whales is *Orcinus orca*. Orcas can be found in any ocean; they are not limited to polar regions as many seal varieties are. The hunting of killer whales was not regulated at the beginning of the twentieth century. Orcas and other whales were usually killed by harpoon. Whale blubber (fat) was harvested and melted down into oil. The oil was used for fuel and to make soap, margarine, wax, varnish, cosmetics, and lubricants for some machinery. The whale bones were used in making products such as fishing rods, umbrella rods, and hoops for women's skirts, among other uses. The unused portions of the whale carcasses were then left on the beaches or sent out to sea.

rest of the men to avoid dampening their spirits. Instead, Shackleton only told the men that they had not progressed as much as expected. When the crew rested on an iceberg that night, the boats bumped perilously against one another. The men had to work through the night to keep the boats apart. They could not afford to lose even one of the boats, as all were needed to carry the 28 men.

By April 13, the crew was haggard. Shackleton knew they needed to reach Elephant Island quickly if they had any hope of survival. He had the men fed extra rations that day; however, some of the men could not enjoy the heartier meal due to seasickness. They shoved off again, and by noon they were finally in open water. This was the good news. The bad news was that the conditions on the boats had worsened and everything was wet except for the dry mouths of the

Weary and Worn-out Men

Shackleton noted the condition of the men in his diary: "Their lips were cracked and their eyes and eyelids showed red in their salt-encrusted faces. The beards even of the younger men might have been those of patriarchs, for the frost and the salt spray had made them white."[6]

thirsty men. They tried sucking on ice that had been brought aboard, but it gave little relief. Chewing on raw seal meat also helped some, but the meat was salty and it increased their thirst terribly. Almost all of the men were frostbitten as well. They needed to reach land quickly.

Land Ho

That night, the *Dudley Docker* went ahead of the other two boats to find a safe place to land. Later, they found each other by shining lights from each of the boats. Explained Worsley, "At 9:30 a.m. we spied a narrow, rocky beach at the base of some very high crags and cliffs, and made for it. . . . We were so delighted that we gave three cheers."[7]

On April 16, they found a safe place to land on the island. This was the first time the men had set foot on actual land for a year and a half since leaving on the expedition from South

The Coldest Place on Earth

In 1983, the lowest temperature in Antarctica was recorded at −128.6 degrees Fahrenheit (−89°C). This remains the lowest recorded temperature anywhere in the world. The highest recorded temperature in Antarctica was 59 degrees Fahrenheit (15°C), taken January 5, 1974. Winds on Antarctica can reach 200 miles per hour (320 km/h)—that is two and a half times the force of a hurricane—and the windchill can lower the temperature dramatically. On the sea surrounding Antarctica, it is slightly warmer, but the men of the *Endurance* were still regularly working in dangerous, below-zero weather.

Georgia Island. Shackleton observed, "They were laughing uproariously, picking up stones and letting handfuls of pebbles trickle between their fingers like misers gloating over hoarded gold."[8]

The men went wild with joy. Geologist James Wordie observed in his diary, "Some fellows were half crazy. One got an axe and did not stop until he had killed about ten seals."[9]

They settled in for a week while Shackleton planned the next and more treacherous journey across the stubborn sea en route to South Georgia Island. ⌒

The expedition braved the icy ocean in this tiny lifeboat and two others.

Shackleton and five others left Elephant Island on April 24, 1915.

SAILING FOR SOUTH GEORGIA

Shackleton started preparing for the next leg of the journey as soon as they landed on Elephant Island. The men rested and planned for the first five days. Then, for the boat journey, Shackleton chose the five men who were in the best condition to travel to South Georgia Island with him: Frank Worsley, whose navigation skills had just proved invaluable; Tom Crean, who had acted heroically on a previous expedition; Chippy McNeish, the carpenter, in case the *James Caird* needed repair; Tim McCarthy, a doctor; and John Vincent. The journey had dauntingly poor odds for success. They would take the *James Caird* because it was the largest of the lifeboats.

Preparing the *James Caird*

McNeish spent the next four days working on the *James Caird*. He used planks from the other two boats to strengthen the deck and covered the top of the hull with canvas. Shackleton wanted the boat covered as much as possible. He knew the men could bail out water, but if too much water filled the boat they could capsize and all would perish. McNeish glued the canvas onto the hull with seal blood. This made it air- and watertight. This covering would also provide a place for the men to sleep at night and shelter from the elements. Thanks to McNeish's ingenuity, the *James Caird* was ready to sail again after only a nine-day break on Elephant Island.

On April 24, they set out. They took four-hour shifts with three men working the sails and rowing while the other three rested under the canvas cover of the deck. The men also ate every four hours to keep up their strength.

The six-man crew in the tiny boat would be tested at every turn. First, gale force winds tossed their boat to and fro, then the boat filled with seawater that had to be constantly bailed out or it would sink. The men battled these conditions for days on the open water. All the while, they had to worry if the wind was forcing them farther away from South Georgia and into the open water of the South Atlantic Ocean.

Worsley used the sextant to take readings of their position. As he did, he had to be balanced by two other men because of the bumpy conditions. If he made a mistake of even one degree in his reading, it would throw their journey off course by 60 miles (100 km). He took four readings during the trip. The rest of his navigation was pure instinct.

The men had been sailing for 12 long days. Just when the weather seemed to be calming, Shackleton spotted the biggest wave he had ever seen. The wave fell over them and swamped the boat. The men bailed furiously, a battle for their very lives, and won.

Landing on the Wrong Side of the Island

On the fifteenth day, kelp and seaweed in the water floated by their boat. These were encouraging signs of land, and they soon spotted South Georgia Island. They had made it! However, they realized they were on the wrong side of the island. They had landed on the south shore, but the settlements at Grytviken and Stromness were on the island's north shore. Shackleton took stock of the *James Caird's* condition. The boat was too weak to make it all the way around the island. They had to land where they were. It was May 10, 1916.

Sextant

In order to navigate across the ocean in the tiny lifeboats, Captain Worsley had to take readings of the sun against the horizon with an instrument known as a sextant. Looking through the sextant, Worsley measured the altitude, which is the height from the water to the sun, in order to determine their position on a map.

A sextant looks like a math protractor because it has an arc. The sextant's arc is one-sixth of a circle. The instrument has a movable metal arm whose angle is adjusted based on the location of the sun, and a sighting hole to locate the horizon. The sextant allowed the ship's navigator Frank Worsley to measure angles and determine the ship's location. Worsely took these measurements in a rocking boat, so it was difficult to get an accurate measurement. He needed the sun to make an accurate measurement, and it was rarely spotted in the overcast weather. Fortunately for the men, Worsley succeeded and his sightings were accurate. The men also used a chronometer on the trip. The chronometer was used mainly for telling time, and it was a less reliable instrument.

The men used a sextant similar to this one to navigate.

There was shelter on the island because of an overhanging cliff. There was also a natural spring from a melting glacier; the parched men drank thirstily. Still, they would have to go over the mountains to reach the whaling stations. Shackleton chose Crean and Worsley to journey across the mountains with him. The others were left behind to wait. Vincent was too ill from the long boat journey to travel, so Shackleton chose him to stay behind with the doctor, McCarthy. Shackleton left McNeish in charge. What lay ahead was a 22-mile (35-km) trek across unknown mountainous territory. The men rested for four days before attempting to go on. To prepare, McNeish put screws on the bottom of the men's shoes for better traction while climbing. They also packed an axe to use to chop steps into the snow.

Getting across South Georgia

Shackleton, Crean, and Worsley left at 2:00 a.m. on May 19 with the moon lighting their way. They packed enough biscuits and rations for three days' travel in spare stockings slung around their necks. They brought the kerosene stove, rope, binoculars, compasses, and the chronometer to tell time. They also had Worsley to lead them through the uncharted region. The navigator had already proved invaluable in getting the men to Elephant Island, and he would be key to their success once again.

The Fourth Man

Shackleton was a religious man. When his men were in Dump Camp deciding what to leave and what to keep, he read to them from the Bible Queen Alexandra had given them. He also believed there was a fourth man with them on the long journey across the South Georgia mountain range, which was their last struggle to get back to civilization. He implied that Jesus Christ was walking with him. "I know that during that long and racking march of 36 hours over the unnamed mountains and glaciers of South Georgia it seemed to me often that we were four, not three. I said nothing to my companions on the point, but afterwards Worsley said to me, 'Boss, I had a curious feeling on the march that there was another person with us.' Crean confessed to the same idea. One feels 'the dearth of human words, the roughness of mortal speech' in trying to describe things intangible."[2]

The mountains were impassable in several places, and the men were forced to backtrack and start again. With daylight disappearing, the men found themselves perilously at the top of a mountain ridge. Being exposed high on the mountain at night was dangerous. They had to get to the bottom of the mountain fast. Worsley recorded in his journal what Shackleton said then, "We've got to take a risk. Are you game?"[1] Shackleton suggested they slide. So the three men formed an interlocking human chain and hurtled down the 1,500-foot (560-m) hill in no time. Once again, their ingenuity had beaten the odds. They shook hands at their successful ride. But it was getting dark, and the men were exhausted from the day's climb. Crean and Worsley huddled in the snow and fell asleep. Shackleton worried the men would die from the cold in their sleep. So he waited only five minutes and then roused the men, telling them they had slept for a half hour so they would feel rested. He urged them to get up and go on.

Next, they found a place to pass through the mountains, but first they decided to stop for a hot breakfast early in the morning of May 20. While Crean heated the stove, Shackleton went to get a better look over the ridge. He heard a faint whistle blowing. If it really was a whistle, it was the whalers' morning wake-up call. Shackleton excitedly shared this news, and the men waited to see if the 7:00 a.m. whistle would blow at the start of the workday. They watched the hands on Worsley's chronometer tick off. The whistle blew. They forgot breakfast and hurried in the direction of the station.

With threadbare clothes and dirty faces, the men stumbled into Stromness Whaling Station. The first people to see them were two young boys who ran away frightened at the sight of the odd-looking, scruffy men. The men went on and knocked on the door to the manager's house.

When the door opened, Shackleton said, "Don't you know me?"

The man replied, "I know your voice."

"My name is Shackleton."

The man immediately led them inside.

"Tell me, when was the war over?" Shackleton asked.

"The war is not over. . . . Millions are being killed. Europe is mad. The world is mad."[3] No one had expected the war to go on so long. The men thought surely it would have ended by then, but it had not.

The men had worn the same clothes since they had lost the *Endurance* and had also not bathed since losing their ship ten months before. Shackleton apologized for their appearance by saying, "I'm afraid we smell."

The manager simply replied, "That doesn't matter. . . . We're used to it on a whaling station."[4]

The station manager immediately sent a boat for the three men on the other side of the island. The men showered, shaved, and ate. They left Stromness and headed for Grytviken Whaling Station. Then Shackleton began planning for the more difficult rescue of the 22 men left on Elephant Island.

Grytviken Whaling Station, South Georgia Island

*The men left behind on Elephant Island sheltered
in the remaining lifeboats.*

THE RESCUE

Frank Wild, Shackleton's second in
command, had been left in charge
on Elephant Island. The men set up shelter by
overturning the two remaining lifeboats, creating
one large covered area they named the Snuggery.

Outside the Snuggery, tents were used to cover the shelter and keep the cold out. Inside the Snuggery, a stove was set up, including a chimney. The whole space was 12.1 feet by 18 feet (3.7 by 5.5 m)—not much room for 22 men to mill about. The ceiling was so low they could not stand up all the way. This new home was dubbed Camp Wild because Frank Wild discovered the area in which they set up camp.

To keep the men's spirits up, Wild kept them on a strict schedule. He had learned this from Shackleton. It was important for the men to have something to focus on, or they could fall into despair or go crazy from waiting and worry.

Following the schedule, the cook started breakfast preparations at 7:00 a.m. each day. By 8:45 a.m., the men were eating penguin steaks. At night, the men sang songs. One of the items rescued from the ship was Leonard Hussey's banjo. This was heavier than the two pounds (1 kg) they had been limited to, but the banjo entertained the men when their spirits needed lifting the most. The weeks turned into months. The men began to worry Shackleton was not coming back.

Elephant Island Daily Menu

- Breakfast: Penguin fried in blubber, drink of water
- Lunch: Biscuits with raw blubber
- Dinner: Penguin, hot drink of Bovril

Four Times to the Rescue

Captain Worsley rode a Norwegian rescue ship to retrieve the three men stuck on the other side of South Georgia. He walked behind the Norwegian sailors, who greeted the men first. "Well, we thought the Skipper would have come back, anyway," McCarthy said. Then Worsley, confused at the men not recognizing him, spoke up, "Well, I am here."[1] Worsley was so clean shaven that the men could not tell it was him.

The rescue from Elephant Island, however, would prove more difficult. Time was of the essence. The men were running out of food, and the pack ice would prove a problem once again.

Shackleton left for the first try at rescue just three days after he had reached civilization at Stromness. Shackleton recruited an old friend named Captain Thom to lead the ship. The rest of the crew consisted of whalers who were anxious to help with the rescue. They took the whaling ship *Southern Sky* and got within 100 miles (160 km) of Elephant Island before the pack ice closed in. They pushed ahead 40 more miles (60 km) before realizing they had to turn back.

After retreating, they went to the Falkland Islands instead of going back to South Georgia. Shackleton also sent telegrams for help from the British Admiralty, the naval affairs office led at the time by Winston Churchill. With World War I still raging, no help was forthcoming. This cable was the first news anyone had heard of Shackleton's expedition in 15 months. The news was immediately published in papers across the globe. But World War I was all consuming, and no one was eager to help the small group of marooned explorers. Unable to muster help from his own countrymen, Shackleton turned to those nearby, asking the countries of Uruguay and Argentina for help. Uruguay sent the ship *Instituto de Pesca No. 1.*

World War I

On August 1, 1914, just as the *Endurance* was getting ready to sail, Germany declared war on Russia, and World War I began. Hearing the news, Shackleton immediately sent a telegram to Admiral Winston Churchill, volunteering the *Endurance*, its stores, and its crew for the war effort. He had just spent seven months planning the expedition and raising money to pay for the ship, crew, and provisions, but was nonetheless willing to help the war effort. Churchill's telegram response said, "Proceed."[2] Churchill phoned soon after and thanked Shackleton for his offer but wished him well, instead, on the expedition. With the blessing of the Admiralty, the *Endurance* Expedition left port.

Some criticized the men of the expedition for leaving when war had begun. However, at the time the expedition left, the war was expected to last only a few months. After the two-year ordeal at sea, the men learned the war was still raging. Even after their harrowing experience on the expedition, many of the crew from the *Endurance* joined the war effort. World War I went on for another two years before ending in 1918.

The Yelcho *rescued the men from Elephant Island.*

Shackleton and the ship got within 20 miles (32 km) of Elephant Island in this second attempt at rescue before pack ice forced them back. When they returned to the Falklands this time, a British Royal Navy ship was in port, the *Glasgow*. The captain of the navy ship sent a telegram to Winston Churchill for permission to attend to the rescue. "Your telegram not approved," was the only response received.[3]

A Long Shot but Worth a Try

With no luck getting help at nearby British-occupied Port Stanley in the Falkland Islands, Shackleton headed to Punta Arenas in Chile. The schooner *Emma* was in port. Shackleton attempted a third rescue in it, again getting within 100 miles (160 km) of Elephant Island before having to turn back. The pack ice was relentless. Next, the Chileans provided Shackleton with a small ship, the *Yelcho*, which looked unable to succeed. His spirits deflated now, Shackleton set off in the *Yelcho* for the fourth and final try. The *Yelcho* was not built to withstand pack ice, but Shackleton was in no position to turn down the little ship as an option for rescue. He was desperate, but he had to stay hopeful.

Meanwhile, the 22 men left behind had now been on Elephant Island for four months—much longer than anyone expected the rescue would take. Despair set over the camp. The men had to eat snails that they pulled from the freezing water.

On August 30, the *Yelcho* sailed through open water and arrived just off Elephant Island. The men were eating a lunch of hoosh when the ship was spotted. Marston was the first to see it. He asked if he should start a fire. The others asked why. "Ship O!"

he yelled.[4] The excited men sprang up and knocked over the hoosh pot, running to signal the ship that they were alive and all was well.

Shackleton counted to see that all 22 were there. He yelled from the ship, "Are you all well?" Wild responded, "All safe, all well."[5]

Worsley recorded this in his journal: "[Shackleton] put his glasses back in their case and turned to me, his face showing more emotion than I had ever known it show before. Crean had joined us, and we were all unable to speak."[6] He noted Shackleton's emotions: "[Shackleton's] face lit up and years seemed to fall off his age."[7]

Concerned that pack ice would trap the *Yelcho*, Shackleton did not even set foot on Elephant Island. He wasted no time in ferrying the men back to the *Yelcho*. Finally, the fourth rescue attempt was a success. Shackleton sent his crew home. Now, he had to find out what had happened to the other party.

This monument on Elephant Island marks the spot where Shackleton's men camped and commemorates the captain of the Yelcho.

The Ross Sea party set sail in the Aurora.

Laying the Depots

eanwhile, the Ross Sea party—the group of men sent to the other side of Antarctica to lay food depots—was in trouble. Shackleton had never lost a life in all of the parties he had been in charge of, but the Ross Sea party was not under Shackleton's charge. The captain of the Ross Sea party and the *Aurora* was Aeneas Mackintosh. He had been with Shackleton on the *Nimrod* in 1907.

On December 24, 1914, three weeks after Shackleton had left port with the *Endurance*, the *Aurora* set sail for the opposite side of Antarctica to lay food depots so Shackleton's men would not starve while making their way across the barren land. The Ross Sea party had no way of learning what was happening on the *Endurance*. They continued their part of the mission as planned, unaware their work would be in vain.

Some of the men in the Ross Sea party went ashore to lay the depots, while the remaining members stayed on board to man the ship. The laying of the depots started at the eightieth parallel—not far from where Scott and his party had died trying to come back from the pole in 1912.

"The air temperature this morning was –35 degrees Fahrenheit [–37°C]. Last night was one of the worst I have ever experienced. To cap everything, I developed toothache, presumably as a result of frostbitten cheek. . . . We have had to reduce our daily ration. Frostbites are frequent in consequence. The surface became very rough in the afternoon, and the light, too, was bad owing to . . . clouds being massed over the sun. . . . Our matches, among other things, are running short, and we have given up using any except for lighting the Primus [stove].[1]

—*Diary entry,*
Captain Mackintosh,
March 15, 1915

On the way, the men of the Ross Sea party laid out markers to find their way back to camps they set up along their route. The main camp was called Cape Evans, where the *Aurora* was docked. The other supply camps were called Hut Point and Safety Camp. Supplies were loaded and moved between the camps, organized, and carried on sledges to the food depots by smaller groups of men from the shore party. Some members of the depot-laying group included Mackintosh; Harry Ernest Wild, brother of Frank Wild from the *Endurance*; Ernest Edward Joyce, a sledging expert; Reverend Arnold Spencer-Smith; Victor George Hayward; and Dick Richards.

Approximately every 60 miles (100 km), the depots were laid in blocks of ice. Tall poles with black flags were stuck out of the top of the ice blocks, so they could be seen from a distance. The journey back

"I shiver in a frozen sleeping-bag. The inside fur is a mass of ice, congealed from my breath. One creeps into the bag, toggles up with half-frozen fingers, and hears the crackling of the ice. Presently drops of thawing ice are falling on one's head. Then comes a fit of shivers. You rub yourself and turn over to warm the side of the bag which has been uppermost. A puddle of water forms under the body. After about two hours you may doze off, but I always wake with the feeling that I have not slept a wink."[2]

—*Diary entry, Captain Mackintosh, March 2, 1915*

Men of the Ross Sea party skied across Antarctica to lay the supply depots.

over Antarctica to reach the shelter of the camps was
treacherous. Wild was frostbitten on the journey;
he had to have a toe amputated and also lost part of
one ear.

Drifting with the *Aurora*

When the shore party arrived back at Cape Evans
on June 2, 1915, the men found that several of
their sled dogs had died. Worse yet, the ship had
disappeared. They found only the broken lines
that had held it onshore. Strong winds had swept
the *Aurora* away on pack ice. "She's gone," Dick

Richards, an Australian physicist, announced. "The ship's gone. The wind has taken her out."[3] Ten men were stranded at Cape Evans. Most of their supplies had been on the ship. Yet they intended to continue their mission and lay the rest of Shackleton's depots.

The drift on the pack ice was similar to what the *Endurance* experienced in the Weddell Sea, but the Ross Sea party and the *Aurora* were on pack ice in the Ross Sea. The crew of the *Aurora* was onboard the ship when it drifted away; the rest of the men had made up the shore party and were left to hope for later rescue. Meanwhile, the *Aurora* drifted helplessly on pack ice for ten months—at the same time, the same thing was happening to the *Endurance* on the other side of the continent. In March 1916, the *Aurora* broke free of the pack ice and was back in open water again.

While this was going on, the shore party stayed on its mission and kept laying depots, assuming the party from the *Endurance* was well on its way across the continent. At one point, Arnold Spencer-Smith became too weakened by scurvy to go on, so he was left in a tent to be picked up along the return trip. Mackintosh and his men continued laying depots.

Later, the men went back and got Spencer-Smith. He could not walk, so they put him in a sleeping bag and strapped him onto a sledge. Farther along in the journey back to Hut Point, which was still 100 miles (160 km) away, Mackintosh and Hayward became unable to walk due to scurvy. They were also picked up and carried back by sledge. Richards, Joyce, and Wild were left to haul the weakened men.

Three men died during the course of the expedition. Spencer-Smith was among those who perished. He died shortly before the party reached Safety Camp. Richards and Wild dug a snowy grave for him. Icicles had already frozen on

Scurvy

Scurvy was a dangerous disease for seamen and polar explorers. It is caused by a lack of vitamin C in the diet. Vitamin C was not understood until the twentieth century, but there is evidence that back in 1747, Scottish doctor James Lind had discovered how to prevent it. By the eighteenth century, sailors had figured out that consuming citrus prevented scurvy, so ships were sent to sea with a store of lime juice. However, sailors still came down with the disease many years later.

When Scott's ship the *Discovery* left, they did not have adequate supplies to stave off scurvy for their entire journey. As a result, Shackleton fell ill to this disease. He tried eating fresh meat, which made the scurvy subside.

On the Scott expedition to the South Pole, nearly every crewmember came down with this dreaded disease, which can turn one's legs black and gums bloody. Eventually, scurvy kills its victims if left untreated. Among the three Ross Sea party deaths, Arnold Spencer-Smith died of cold and scurvy near the Ross Ice Shelf. Other expedition members suffered from the disease but recovered.

his beard and eyelashes. They marked the grave with a cross made of sticks.

Daylight on the continent was gone by mid-March, and the men were steeped in 24 hours of darkness with their only light from candles they burned. The only food they had to eat was seal meat. They used oil from the meat for cooking fuel. The bright side of this was that the fresh meat cured Mackintosh and Hayward of their scurvy. This reenergized the two men, and they decided that travel to Cape Evans, a camp with better food and accommodations, was possible on May 8. However, their colleagues Richards, Wild, and Joyce were against this, saying that a blizzard was eminent. Joyce even said, "You may call me 'old cautious' but I would not go to Cape Evans today for all the tea in China."[4]

Mackintosh and Hayward ignored the warnings and went on their way. But the blizzard did strike as Joyce

Sunlight in a Desert of Ice

For half of the year, Antarctica sits in darkness. The Antarctic summer runs from December to March each year. When summer arrives, the sun appears and lights up the surface of Antarctica. But even though the sun is there, most of the heat generated reflects back into the atmosphere and does not warm the continent.

predicted, and Mackintosh and Hayward were never heard from again. It is assumed they were killed in the extreme weather or fell through the ice.

The blizzard raged on while Richards, Wild, and Joyce stayed trapped in their tent. In mid-July, they began the trek to Cape Evans. They were shaken momentarily when the moon dimmed and all around them the light slowly faded. Wondering if it was the end of the world, they looked up and saw there was no cause for concern, as they witnessed a full eclipse of the moon. Eventually, they reached Cape Evans and safety, reuniting with the other four expedition members.

Waiting at Cape Evans

Shackleton had not forgotten the men of the Ross Sea party. Early in December 1917, the *Aurora* was repaired and docked in Port Chalmers in New Zealand, where Shackleton met up with the ship. On December 20, Shackleton set sail with the *Aurora* to rescue the men left behind at Cape Evans. Shackleton's old friend Captain John K. Davis, who was with Shackleton on his first expedition from 1907 to 1909, was placed in charge of the *Aurora* and Captain Davis selected a crew of men to go with them on this final rescue. The men of the Ross Sea party knew Shackleton's reputation and had confidence that he would eventually come rescue them, but they had no idea when.

Rescue finally came on January 10, 1917. "There's a ship out there," said Richards.[5] The men ran out to see it—the *Aurora* really had come back to retrieve them. Shackleton and two men went to the camp and then signaled the *Aurora* by laying flat on the ice. This was a signal they had agreed on to tell those back on the *Aurora* how many men had died. Three members of the Ross Sea party perished, Captain Mackintosh included, who had turned out to be less cautious than Shackleton who had hired him. ⌐

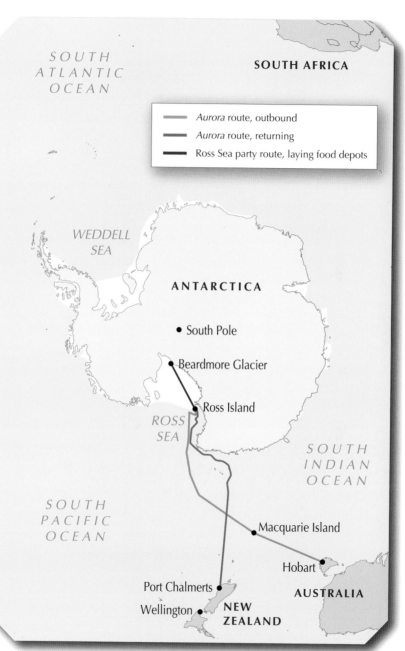

SOUTH
ATLANTIC
OCEAN

SOUTH AFRICA

Aurora route, outbound
Aurora route, returning
Ross Sea party route, laying food depots

WEDDELL
SEA

ANTARCTICA

● South Pole

● Beardmore Glacier

● Ross Island

ROSS
SEA

SOUTH
INDIAN
OCEAN

SOUTH
PACIFIC
OCEAN

● Macquarie Island

Hobart

Port Chalmerts

AUSTRALIA

Wellington

NEW
ZEALAND

Route of the Ross Sea party

Shackleton leaving on his final expedition, September 1921

ONE LAST VOYAGE

fter returning from Antarctica, Shackleton volunteered his services to the war effort. He was turned down for active duty because he refused to undergo a physical examination. Shackleton knew he had a bad heart, which would disqualify him from future adventures as an explorer if word got out.

Finally, he was given a diplomatic post in Buenos Aires. He was supposed to persuade the Chilean and Argentinean governments to join the Allies in the war effort. However, the two countries remained neutral rather than take sides in the conflict. The war ended in 1918.

GOING SOUTH

When the war ended, Shackleton wrote his memoir *South* about the *Endurance* Expedition with the help of writer Edward Saunders. Shackleton dictated most of the book, and Saunders helped shape the book. Shackleton always felt he was a better speaker than writer, and he loved telling stories of his Antarctic adventures. However, his speaking engagements were not as well attended as they once had been. He was bored and restless; he needed to go south again. Shackleton began plans for another expedition and started raising funds. But he did not have a clear goal for the expedition, except to propose that he would circumnavigate Antarctica and look for islands not yet discovered. Shackleton's college classmate John Quiller Rowett financed the expedition. Hence, it was named the Shackleton-Rowett Expedition.

By 1921, Shackleton had purchased the Norwegian sealing ship *Foca 1*. He renamed the ship the *Quest*. Even without a clear goal for the expedition, eight men who had served with Shackleton previously signed on: the meteorologist Leonard Hussey, the surgeon Alexander Macklin, the engineer A. J. Kerr, the cook Charles Green, seaman Thomas McLeod, surgeon James McIlroy, second in command Frank Wild, and the *Endurance*'s Captain Frank Worsley.

But Shackleton's health was failing. The *Quest* sailed to Cumberland Bay in South Georgia and anchored there, which was near the whaling station where the *Endurance* had set sail. It was January 4, 1922. Shackleton enjoyed one last night reuniting with comrades from eight years prior. Early the next morning on January 5, he had a heart attack and died. Shackleton was only 47 years old.

"For a joint scientific and geographical piece of organization, give me Scott; . . . for a dash to the Pole and nothing else, Amundsen: and if I am in the devil of a hole and want to get out of it, give me Shackleton every time. They will all go down in polar history as leaders, these men."[1]

—*Polar explorer Apsley Cherry-Garrard, a member of Robert Falcon Scott's last expedition*

Shackleton's body was loaded and shipped on a whaling boat. When the *Quest* docked in Montevideo, Uruguay, the crew received word from Shackleton's wife, Emily, to send him back to South Georgia Island. She wanted him to be buried among the whalers, near the land he loved so much. On March 5, 1922, Shackleton was buried at Grytviken Whaling Station.

Shackleton's death is considered the last fatality in the string of 21 men who died in Antarctica from 1897 to 1922 during the so-called Heroic Age of Exploration. Many of the men died of scurvy or cold. Four of the deaths were due not to Antarctic exposure but to other diseases.

The Antarctic Treaty

Antarctica is the only continent in the world that is not governed by a specific country. Even though the South Pole was claimed by Norwegian Roald Amundsen, Norway does not claim Antarctica as its territory. The area is governed by a treaty. This document was written and signed by 12 countries to set up regulations for conducting scientific experiments there. The treaty was signed in Washington DC on December 1, 1959.

The original 12 countries were: Argentina, Australia, Belgium, Chile, the French Republic, Japan, New Zealand, Norway, the Union of South Africa, the Union of Soviet Socialist Republics, the United Kingdom of Great Britain and Northern Ireland, and the United States of America. Since 1959, many additional governments have signed on. By signing the treaty, the countries agree to use Antarctica only in peaceful ways, such as to increase scientific knowledge.

THE LEGACY OF THE *ENDURANCE*

Shackleton and the *Endurance* Expedition have been the subject of numerous books. Even today, news of Shackleton makes headlines, whether it is a discovery of an old stockpile of whiskey or the remains of shelters found by other explorers.

Shackleton's legacy was not the success of his explorations but the failures. He never reached the South Pole as his comrades Scott and Amundsen did. Shackleton also failed to complete the goal of the Imperial Trans-Antarctic Expedition, which was to cross Antarctica from coast to coast. This would be completed 50 years later by explorer Vivian Fuchs with a group that included the famous climber of Mount Everest Sir Edmund Hillary.

After returning from the *Endurance* Expedition, Shackleton wrote this in his memoir:

Crossing Antarctica

Sir Edmund Hillary was a member of the first team to achieve what Shackleton had set out to do with the *Endurance*, crossing the Antarctic continent going from shore to shore. Hillary completed this feat in 1958 as part of an expedition led by fellow explorer Vivian Fuchs. They had the use of motorized cars, whereas Shackleton did not have that technology. Hillary is more famous for being the first person, with partner Tenzing Norgay, to reach the top of Mount Everest, Earth's highest mountain, in 1953.

That was all of tangible things; but in memories we were rich. We had pierced the veneer of outside things. We had 'suffered, starved and triumphed, grovelled [sic] down yet grasped at glory, grown bigger in the bigness of the whole.' We had seen God in His splendours, heard the text that Nature renders. We had reached the naked soul of man. [2]

He was quoting some of his favorite lines from the poem "The Call of the Wild," by Robert Service, published in his book *The Spell of the Yukon and Other Verses*.

Shackleton's granddaughter Alexandra Shackleton envisioned how the men felt upon reaching civilization after their long struggle:

They had accomplished what many regard as the greatest small boat journey in the world, 800 miles [1300 km] across the stormiest seas in the world in a little boat not even 23 feet [7 m] long—all the while encountering extremely harsh

Exploration Then and Now

After the *Endurance* Expedition, many others have traveled to Antarctica. In fact, as many as 30 tourist ships travel to Antarctica each year to explore the coldest place on Earth and see its natural inhabitants, such as orcas, Weddell seals, and 17 varieties of penguins.

In 2008, when Werner Herzog landed on Antarctica in a plane to film his nature documentary *Encounters at the End of the World*, the plane was met by a huge bus weighing 67,000 pounds with oversized snow tires. Herzog said that he was "surprised to find McMurdo [research station] looking like an ugly mining town filled with Caterpillars and noisy construction sites." [3] According to the documentary, approximately 1,000 people live on Antarctica.

weather and suffering gales, privations of thirst, hunger, and everything. It was a colossal achievement, and when they saw the black peaks of South Georgia, they felt huge relief and happiness.[4]

Where Shackleton succeeded was in valuing the lives of his men above all else and ensuring that everyone came home alive. The success of Shackleton and his men is often described as a triumph of the human spirit. They faced the worst circumstances and obstacles, but they never gave up. This is the legacy that endures.

To the memory of
ERNEST·HENRY
SHACKLETON
EXPLORER

Born
15ᵗʰ Feb. 1874
Entered Life Eternal
5ᵗʰ Jan. 1922

This monument marks Shackleton's grave in South Georgia.

TIMELINE

1874	1901	1907
Ernest Shackleton is born on February 15.	Shackleton leaves with Robert Falcon Scott's *Discovery* Expedition July 31. He is sent home in 1903 after he contracts scurvy.	In August, Shackleton's *Nimrod* Expedition leaves England.

1914	1914	1914
On August 1, World War I begins.	The *Endurance* leaves Plymouth, England, on August 8.	On December 5, the *Endurance* departs South Georgia Island, the last stop before heading for Antarctica.

1909

On January 9, Shackleton's *Nimrod* Expedition gets within 100 miles (160 km) of the South Pole.

1911

On December 14, Norwegian Roald Amundsen is the first explorer to reach the South Pole.

1912

In March, Scott and four of his party members die returning from the South Pole.

1914

On December 24, the *Aurora* sets sail for the Ross Sea side of Antarctica.

1915

The *Endurance* gets stuck in pack ice on the Weddell Sea on January 19.

1915

On June 2, the Ross Sea party led by Aeneas Mackintosh returns from laying depots to find the *Aurora* has disappeared.

TIMELINE

1915	1915	1916
On October 27, the *Endurance* is crushed by ice and starts to break up.	On November 21, the *Endurance* sinks.	On April 9, all 28 men leave for Elephant Island in the three small lifeboats.

1916	1916	1916
On May 10, the *James Caird* lands on the uninhabited side of South Georgia Island.	On May 20, Shackleton and two men reach Stromness Whaling Station.	On August 30, the 22 men on Elephant Island are rescued by Shackleton and the small Chilean ship *Yelcho*.

1916

On April 16, all three lifeboats land safely on Elephant Island.

1916

The *James Caird*, the largest lifeboat, is launched on April 24, heading for South Georgia Island with six men.

1916

On May 8, Hayward and Mackintosh of the Ross Sea party die, bringing the total of deaths from their expedition to three.

1917

On January 10, Shackleton and the *Aurora* return to rescue the remaining men of the Ross Sea party.

1918

World War I ends on November 11.

1922

On January 5, Shackleton dies of a heart attack on South Georgia Island.

Essential Facts

Date of Event

August 8, 1914, to January 10, 1917

Place of Event

South Georgia Island

Weddell Sea

Ross Sea

Elephant Island

Key Players

❖ Winston Churchill

❖ Frank Hurley

❖ The Ross Sea party

❖ Sir Ernest Shackleton

❖ The Weddell Sea party

❖ Frank Arthur Worsley

❖ Frank Wild

Highlights of Event

❖ The objective of the *Endurance* Expedition was to cross Antarctica from sea to sea, starting at the Weddell Sea and landing on the continent, then crossing over until they reached the Ross Sea on the other side of Antarctica.

❖ The crew of the *Endurance* never set foot on land because their ship became trapped in an ice floe early in their journey. As a result, the crew and the ship drifted on the ice for ten months, expecting their ship would eventually break free of the ice.

❖ Eventually, they abandoned their mission and sought a place to launch the lifeboats and save their lives. They made it safely to nearby Elephant Island.

❖ From Elephant Island, a smaller rescue party of six took one lifeboat on a treacherous ocean journey. The six landed on the uninhabited side of South Georgia Island. From there, three men trudged over the mountains in blizzard conditions and made it back to civilization.

❖ After four attempts with different ships, the rescuers finally broke through the pack ice and reached the 22 men left on Elephant Island. All of the men of the Weddell Sea party lived, making it one of the most famous rescue stories in history.

❖ The Ross Sea party completed its mission of laying supply depots for the main party. It lost three men as it was trapped on the continent for almost two years.

Quote

"Men go out into the void spaces of the world for various reasons . . . love of adventure . . . thirst for scientific knowledge, and . . . the mysterious fascination of the unknown."—*Sir Ernest Shackleton*

Glossary

capsize
> To turn over.

chronometer
> A device used for taking exact measurements of time and longitudes at sea.

crag
> A steep rock or ledge.

crest
> White beard or top of a wave; the highest point or summit.

depot
> A station or place to leave supplies.

fortitude
> Mental ability to withstand difficult times and situations.

hoosh
> A thick stew sometimes made with suet or biscuits, fat, and dried meat.

hull
> The frame or body of a ship.

ice floe
> Floating ice that measures less than 6 miles (10 km).

ice shelf
> Flat platform on top of a glacier.

longitude
> Measurement in degrees of east and west distance on Earth.

morale
> Mental ability of the crew to withstand hardship.

pack ice
> Big and small pieces of broken ice.

perilous
> Having risk of danger.

perish
> To die or be ruined.

provisions

Supplies such as food and clothing.

scurvy

A frequent disease or affliction of sailors due to lack of vitamin C.

sextant

Device used to determine latitude and longitude by measuring sun angles.

sledge

A sled for carrying supplies and usually pulled by sled dogs.

stern

The back of the ship.

ADDITIONAL RESOURCES

SELECTED BIBLIOGRAPHY

Alexander, Caroline. *The Endurance: Shackleton's Legendary Antarctic Expedition.* New York: Knopf, 1998. Print.

Capparell, Stephanie, and Margot Morrell. *Shackleton's Way.* New York: Viking, 2001. Print.

Hurley, Frank. *South with Endurance: Shackleton's Antarctic Expedition 1914–1917—The Photographs of Frank Hurley.* London: Simon, 2001. Print.

Shackleton, Ernest. *The Heart of the Antarctic.* Edinburgh: Birlinn Limited, 2000. Print.

Shackleton, Ernest. *South.* First Edition. New York: Carroll, 1998. Print.

Worsley, Frank Arthur. *Shackleton's Boat Journey.* Santa Barbara, CA: Narrative, 2001. Print.

FURTHER READINGS

Bancroft, Ann, and Nancy Loewen. *Four to the Pole! The American Women's Expedition to Antarctica, 1992–93.* Northhaven, CT: Linnet, 2001. Print.

Currie, Stephen. *History Makers: Polar Explorers.* San Diego, CA: Lucent, 2002. Print.

McKernan, Victoria. *Shackleton's Stowaway.* New York: Laurel-Leaf, 2005. Print.

Web Links

To learn more about the *Endurance* Expedition, visit ABDO Publishing Company online at **www.abdopublishing.com**. Web sites about the *Endurance* Expedition are featured on our Book Links page. These links are routinely monitored and updated to provide the most current information available.

Places to Visit

American Museum of Natural History
Central Park West at Seventy-Ninth Street, New York, NY 10024
212-769-5100
www.amnh.org/exhibitions/shackleton/exhibition.html
A traveling exhibition features Frank Hurley's photos and film footage, the *James Caird* lifeboat, sextants used for navigation, and other artifacts.

Beargrease Annual Sled Dog Marathon
Beargrease Office, PO Box 500 Duluth, MN 55801
218-722-7631
www.beargrease.com
Every January, a sled dog marathon takes place in Duluth, Minnesota. This is open to the public and includes many fun and educational activities.

Smithsonian Institution
PO Box 37012, MRC 94, Washington, DC 20013-7012
202-633-3168
www.sites.si.edu/exhibitions/exhibits/wondrous/main.htm
The Smithsonian features the traveling exhibit *Wondrous Cold: An Antarctic Journey*.

South Georgia Island and the South Sandwich Islands
www.sgisland.gs
Each year 30 ships tour the islands. Shackleton's grave can be seen near the Grytviken Whaling Station.

SOURCE NOTES

Chapter 1. On Thin Ice

1. "Sir E. Shackleton's Expedition." *Times* [London]. Times Newspapers, 3 Aug. 1914.Web. 11 Oct. 2010.

2. "The Endurance: Shackleton's Legendary Antarctic Exploration." *American Museum of Natural History*. American Museum of Natural History, 2001. Web. 11 Oct. 2010.

3. *The Endurance: Shackleton's Legendary Antarctic Expedition*. Screenplay by Caroline Alexander and Joseph Dorman. Dir. George Butler. Sony Pictures, 2003. DVD.

4. George Plimpton. *Biography: Ernest Shackleton*. New York: DK, 2003. Print. 57–58.

5. *The Endurance: Shackleton's Legendary Antarctic Expedition*. Screenplay by Caroline Alexander and Joseph Dorman. Dir. George Butler. Sony Pictures, 2003. DVD.

6. "Ernest Shackleton's Endurance Diary, 1915." *Scott Polar Research Institute*. Cambridge University, 1915. Web. 1 Aug. 2010.

7. Ernest Shackleton. *South*. First Edition. New York: Carroll, 1998. Print. 66.

8. Ibid. 99.

9. Ibid. 99–100.

10. Ibid. 100.

11. Ibid. 76.

Chapter 2. The Boss

1. Margot Morrell and Stephanie Capparell. *Shackleton's Way*. New York: Viking, 2001. Print. 17.

2. Ibid. 13.

3. George Plimpton. *Biography: Ernest Shackleton*. New York: DK, 2003. Print. 51.

4. Margot Morrell and Stephanie Capparell. *Shackleton's Way*. New York: Viking, 2001. Print. xvi.

Chapter 3. Organizing the Expedition

1. Sir Ernest Shackleton. *The Heart of the Antarctic*. Edinburgh: Birlinn Limited, 2000. Print. 1.

2. Caroline Alexander. *The Endurance: Shackleton's Legendary Antarctic Expedition*. London: Knopf, 1998. Print. 10.

3. Kelly Tyler-Lewis. *The Lost Men: The Harrowing Saga of Shackleton's Ross Sea Party*. New York: Penguin, 2006. Print. 21.

Chapter 4. Camping on the Ice

1. Ernest Shackleton. *South*. First Edition. New York: Carroll, 1998. Print. 83.

2. Ibid. 80.

3. Ibid. 94.

4. Ibid. 105.

5. Ibid. 109.

6. Ibid. 115–116.

7. Ibid. 232–233.

8. Ibid. 91–92.

Chapter 5. Off to Elephant Island

1. "Shackleton's Voyage of Endurance: Diary of a Survivor." *Nova Online*. PBS, 2002. Web. 11 Oct. 2010.

2. Ernest Shackleton. *South*. First Edition. New York: Carroll, 1998. Print. 125–126.

3. Ibid. 131.

4. Ibid. 129.

5. Frank Arthur Worsley. *Shackleton's Boat Journey*. Santa Barbara, CA: Narrative, 2001. Print. 36.

6. Ernest Shackleton. *South*. First Edition. New York: Carroll, 1998. Print. 135.

7. Ibid. 143.

8. Ibid. 145.

9. *The Endurance: Shackleton's Legendary Antarctic Expedition*. Screenplay by Caroline Alexander and Joseph Dorman. Dir. George Butler. Sony Pictures, 2003. DVD.

Source Notes Continued

Chapter 6. Sailing for South Georgia

1. *The Endurance: Shackleton's Legendary Antarctic Expedition.* Screenplay by Caroline Alexander and Joseph Dorman. Dir. George Butler. Sony Pictures, 2003. DVD.

2. Ernest Shackleton. *South.* First Edition. New York: Carroll, 1998. Print. 211.

3. Ibid. 208.

4. George Plimpton. *Biography: Ernest Shackleton.* New York: DK, 2003. Print. 57–106.

Chapter 7. The Rescue

1. Frank Arthur Worsley. *Shackleton's Boat Journey.* Santa Barbara, CA: Narrative, 2001. Print. 145.

2. Ernest Shackleton. *South.* First Edition. New York: Carroll, 1998. Print. xiv.

3. George Plimpton. *Biography: Ernest Shackleton.* New York: DK, 2003. Print. 57–121.

4. Margery and James Fisher. *Shackleton.* London: James Barrie, 1957. Print. 374.

5. Ibid. 375.

6. Caroline Alexander. *The Endurance: Shackleton's Legendary Antarctic Expedition.* London: Knopf, 1998. Print. 183.

7. Frank Arthur Worsley. *Shackleton's Boat Journey.* Santa Barbara, CA: Narrative, 2001. Print. 149.

8. Ernest Shackleton. *South.* First Edition. New York: Carroll, 1998. Print. 241.

Chapter 8. Laying the Depots

1. Ernest Shackleton. *South*. First Edition. New York: Carroll, 1998. Print. 260–261.

2. Ibid. 257.

3. George Plimpton. *Biography: Ernest Shackleton*. New York: DK, 2003. Print. 127.

4. Ibid. 132.

5. Ibid. 134.

Chapter 9. One Last Voyage

1. Sara Wheeler. *Cherry: A Life of Apsley Cherry-Garrard*. New York: Random House, 2003. *Google Book Search*. Web. 11 Oct. 2010.

2. Ernest Shackleton. *South*. First Edition. New York: Carroll, 1998. Print. 207.

3. *Encounters at the End of the World*. Dir. Werner Herzog. Discovery Films, 2008. DVD.

4. "Shackleton's Voyage of Endurance: Tending Sir Ernest's Legacy: An Interview with Alexandra Shackleton." *Nova Online*. PBS, 2002. Web. 11 Oct. 2010.

INDEX

ABOUT THE AUTHOR

Kristin Johnson teaches college writing and lives in Minnesota. Johnson has won several writing awards including the Loose-leaf Poetry Series Award, The Loft's Shabo Award for in-progress picture books, and the Mystery Writers of America Helen McCloy Award. She enjoys reading and traveling, and she is currently working on a novel.

PHOTO CREDITS

Popperfoto/Getty Images, cover, 3; Topical Press Agency/Getty Images, 6, 96 (bottom); Royal Geographic, 10, 14, 38, 60, 70, 74, 81, 98 (top), 98 (bottom); Red Line Editorial, 17, 87; Press Association/AP Images, 18, 96 (top); Hulton Archive/Getty Images, 22, 97; AP Images, 27; North Wind Picture Archives, 28; Topical Press Agency/Getty Images, 33; George F. Mobley/National Geographic/Getty Images, 37; Hulton Archive/Getty Images, 43; Underwood & Underwood/Time & Life Pictures/Getty Images, 49; Jacynth Roode/iStockphoto, 50, 99; Mogens Trolle/iStockphoto, 53; Mansell/Mansell/Time & Life Pictures/Getty Images, 59; Bernard Maurin/Fotolia, 64; Alexander Hafemann/iStockphoto, 69; John Warburton-Lee Photography/Photolibrary, 77; Getty Images, 78; Topical Press Agency/Getty Images, 88; Oxford Scientific/Photolibrary, 95